BEATING BURNOUT:

An Athlete's Guide To

Relentless Recovery

by

Josiah Igono, PhD

Note To Readers:

This publication contains opinions and ideas of its author. It is sold with the understanding that neither the author nor the publisher is engaged in rendering medical diagnoses. If the reader requires such advice or services, a competent professional should be consulted. The strategies outlined in this book may not be suitable for every individual, and are not guaranteed or warranted to produce any particular results. This book is written as a source of information only. The information contained herein should by no means be considered a substitute for the advice of a qualified medical professional, who should always be consulted before beginning any new program.

All efforts have been made to ensure the accuracy of the information contained in this book as of the date published. Due to the changing nature of the Internet, some web links or addresses may have been updated or changed since the time of publication, and may no longer be valid. The author and the publisher expressly disclaim responsibility for any adverse effects arising from the use or application of the information contained herein.

About the Author

Josiah Igono loves helping people establish foundations and frameworks for a powerful mindset.

He is regularly requested by the media, coaches, and professional athletes. The biggest benefits for those he serves are helping performers find purpose, gain clarity, and build confidence as they discover and attack their life's work. For the lion's share of his professional life, Josiah has been knee-deep in the world of athletics, serving as a Strength Coach, Performance Psychology professional, and as a Chaplain. His reach has influenced people globally, and his impact has been felt within professional sports organizations, universities, and in the private sector.

As a former athlete himself, he understands the triumphs and tribulations that performers face; more importantly, the people and environments that go into those equations. Fascinated by how individuals respond to stressors, Josiah has dedicated years to researching mental toughness and the impact it has on athletes and high performers.

He holds his doctorate in Performance Psychology and regularly teaches on various areas of performance.

Josiah and his wife, Erin, reside in Phoenix, AZ with their children Hannah, Michael, Elise, and Justin.

~ ~ ~

To all who are struggling…and to those seeking an edge:

"If your output is greater than your intake, then your upkeep will be your downfall"

-Anonymous

Table of Contents:

How Are You Filling Your Buckets Today?

-A Performance Based Approach to Mental Health-

BIOLOGICAL

SLEEP MEDS MASSAGE GENETIC IQ*

PSYCHOLOGICAL

READING MEDITATION PRAYER JOURNALING

ENVIRONMENTAL

DECOR SUNLIGHT NATURE QUIET ZONES

1/2

*KNOWLEDGE OF FAMILY HEALTH HISTORY

How Are You Filling Your Buckets Today?

-A Performance Based Approach to Mental Health-

BIOLOGICAL

DEEP BREATHING — EXERCISE — PMR* — NUTRITION — HYDRATION

PSYCHOLOGICAL

MUSIC — LAUGHTER — ENTERTAINMENT — PLAY — HOBBIES

ENVIRONMENTAL

FAMILY TIME — LIVING SPACES — SAFETY — RELATIONSHIPS — LOVE

*PROGRESSIVE MUSCLE RELAXATION

2/2

2 Acronyms That Will Make This Book Come To Life

A.I.M. - Within the world of sports, the word 'goals' has been thrown around a lot. The problem with this is that when words are used often, but not defined, the same words lose their meaning and power. In this book, you are going to be challenged to switch from using the word goals to using the word *aim*. When you aim at something, the chances of you hitting your target are heightened. Conversely, when you aim at nothing, you'll get nothing every time! So whatever you desire to achieve, make sure it checks at least 1 of the following boxes:

Actionable: Every goal/desire should be actionable. This means that there must be a physical activity or component that is involved. Because goals are situated in the future, it's very easy for us to *talk* or *overthink* ourselves out of performing the actions that are necessary.

Intentional: For you to have a legitimate goal or desire to be accomplished, there must be intent. This means that this desire will not repeatedly happen on its own. You must do the honorable, yet difficult, work of executing the actions (above) that will lead you to your ultimate destination.

Measurable: Now that you have action items and intent behind what you're aiming to achieve, you can proceed to measure them. We can measure our aim by using different variables, such as time, frequency, duration, intensity, volume, load, etc. Everything that you're measuring should be trackable from beginning, to middle, to its end. Famed business mogul, Peter Drucker, has been quoted as saying, "You cannot manage what you cannot measure." Although this may not be true of all things, it is true of most things.

B.U.R.N. -The opposite of burnout is *relentless recovery*. In a world where athletes are overreaching and overexerting, the complete 180 of this behavior is relentless recovery. Relentless recovery entails aiming at filling your buckets to the best of your capability so that you are able to perform at high levels. So how can you tell if you are burned out, or possibly on the brink of burnout? The following four areas are good indicators (especially if you have been experiencing these areas for multiple weeks) that you may need to engage in relentless recovery.

Boredom or Lack of Motivation: If you are in a high-performing environment and feel bored, are lacking motivation for the things that you once loved and could do incessantly all day, you may want to engage in relentless recovery.

Unusual Fatigue or Exhaustion: If your body is not responding the way it once did, and you are having an inability to bounce back, you should take note. If you are always feeling tired or fatigued with things that usually were a joy to do at one point, you may want to engage in relentless recovery.

Reduced Performance or Productivity: If your performance on the field, court, or whatever your domain of competition lies has plummeted, you should be on the alert. If you look at your statistics, your averages, or your usual marks of performance and they have fallen below standard, more specifically your own norms, you may want to engage in relentless recovery.

Negativity or Negative Outlook: If your attitude is generally negative and you maintain a gloomy disposition, you should rethink these behaviors. Negativity directly impacts neurochemistry, and prolonged patterns of behavior in this state are not advised. If this sounds like you, you may want to engage in relentless recovery.

Some Quick Notes

One Tank

We only have one tank. Our humanity is comprised of our body, mind, and spirit. The essence of our being is encapsulated into this one tank. Everything matters, right? Our inputs matter because they determine our outputs. What we think, eat, drink, listen to, and watch matter. The environment that we are around is also important; everything matters. You are one human; you only have one tank. Knowing this information, why would you intentionally apply yourself to something negative? Or, why would you deliberately allow someone or something negative to continually drain you? Why would you do that? Why would you apply your energy towards excuse-making or whining? Why would you do that, knowing that you only have one tank?

Scientifically Impossible to Plant & Reap

We are all aware that it is scientifically impossible for a seed to be planted in the ground one day and for a fully grown tree to pop up the next day, right? That is not how nature works; it's not the way things operate. That is scientifically impossible. Once we understand this concept, we can apply it to every area of our lives. Most things take time. We have to follow a process, and it cannot be violated. That's why it's so important to get your seeds in the ground right now. Get your seeds in the ground, then water, fertilize, and nurture them. The sun will shine when it's ready. The rain will pour when it's ready. However, it's our job to make sure that we take care of those seeds. It's our job to make sure we get those seeds in the ground. It's our job to do everything that we can in the process before we bear fruit. In doing so, we will reap the harvest in due time.

The Power of Habit

Some scientists posit that we may spend about 90+ percent of each day repeating certain behaviors. In other words, the majority of our days are spent doing the same thing every day! If we are not happy with our lives, the way things are turning out in terms of our outputs, we just need to make minor adjustments to see massive change. This book will provide you with many options.

Output is Greater Than Your Intake

*If your output is greater than your intake, then your upkeep will be your downfall…*This book was written to give you several ways to increase your intake so that you are ready to recover, and to perform from a place of power.

Preface

The opposite of burnout is *relentless recovery*. Burnout is a constant overreaching and overexertion that many athletes encounter, whereas relentless recovery is the complete opposite of this phenomenon. It is continuously pursuing ways in which we can fill our buckets and have fuel in the tank to refuel from the rigors of competition, and to perform from a place of power.

Mental health has become a buzz word in modern day vernacular. We are now seeing more vulnerability in this area than any point in history, particularly with athletes. This book will address what mental health is, why it is important, and how to maintain a healthy mindset. It is not what you may think.

One of the common definitions of health is, *the state of being free from illness or injury*. Furthermore, mental health is defined as a continuum ranging from having good mental health to having a mental disorder. In theory, an individual who is mentally healthy is someone whose mind is somewhat free from anything that would cause it harm or danger. It is important to understand these definitions on a granular level, because 'mental health' is sometimes viewed as a negative construct.

Viewing mental health as simply a negative construct is an injustice because it inhibits people from getting the help they may need. Moreover, it prevents individuals from improving their current position regardless of where they are on the continuum.

For many athletes, prolonged bouts of psychological stress may affect overall mental health. There are various forms of stress (eustress, chronic stress, acute stress, distress, etc.). The appropriate application of stress causes growth; whereas, an overload of stress can cause damage, brokenness, or worse. It is important for athletes to be able to think clearly and manage their moods, emotions, and feelings. Stress is closely related to psychological well-being, and when compromised, can be a detriment to one's mental health.

Various elements, such as an athlete's support system, home life, nutrition, hydration, relationships, medication (if necessary), spirituality, and his or her ability to healthily recover from the rigors of professional and personal responsibilities are vital. Some models in literature, such as the *biopsychosocial model*, first developed by George Engel, suggest that when these disparate areas are addressed, it will yield an individual who is mentally healthy.

Mental health is a complex phenomenon, and a complex model such as the biopsychosocial model may be beneficial in addressing mental health issues that many athletes face. This model may add value in restoring balance for athletes, as it incorporates elements that positively influence one's biology, psychology, and environment.

You will notice an irony about this book. The term 'mental health' is not used one time within the body of this book. This book was written in such a way where you can take several elements using the biopsychosocial model to evaluate how well you have filled these proverbial buckets. One cannot simply go to the marketplace and "buy" health. Health is a byproduct of all of the things that you have, or have not, engaged in beforehand.

Mental health works the same way. The biopsychosocial model is a robust framework in which an athlete can use to dominate their competitive landscape.

-Josiah Igono, PhD

Part I

Biological

After reading this section, you should be able to:

- ✓ explain why addressing human biology is important for recovery

- ✓ recognize why sleep and other functions such as diaphragmatic breathing globally affect human recovery

- ✓ list several means whereby an athlete can physically recover from the rigors of training and competition

- ✓ administer several techniques that have immediate impact on human recovery

Sleep

It goes without saying that sleep is the new currency. In our hyper-connected world, with production and presence being at a premium, it is no wonder that people go non-stop. We grind. We hustle. We work our fingers to the bone without taking into account the ramifications of our actions. When you don't sleep, you're basically stealing from yourself. Sometimes athletes are the worst culprits. If you don't get your sleep, you will pay a heavy price.

The deleterious effects of a lack of sleep have been shown in research to increase anxiety in athletes, and has been correlated to individuals with depression. This ultimately affects athletic performance. Yes, genetically there are some people who require more sleep (or less) than others. Chances are, however, that this is an argument you want to stay away from. The restorative benefits of sleep impact nearly every function in the human body. Whether we are talking about memory, the physiological benefits of exercise, digestion, or even psychological stress, sufficient sleep has positive implications on human performance. There are many sleep aids, sleep apps, and books on sleep. Whatever you do, get sleep.

Sleep education is not as prevalent for athletes as one may think. Although it is a part of life and how we survive, many in the athletic world simply take it for granted. There are many studies that have shown time and time again the correlation between sleep and athletic performance. This becomes even more important when athletes begin to travel across time zones, and internal clocks and rhythms are directly affected.

The benefits and functions of sleep are vast, and when we healthily engage in sleep, our bodies initiate the processes of growing, replacing and removing damaged cells, releasing important hormones, cleaning out toxins, and the list goes on. Our brains begin to consolidate thoughts, solve problems, and with the aid of cerebrospinal fluid, remove toxins and plaque build-up in the brain.

Whereas adequate sleep is necessary for normal brain functioning, optimal sleep is a prerequisite to excellent brain functioning and optimal performance.

I currently grade myself (1-5…1 is terrible, 5 is excellent): _____

My desired grade is: _____

Some things I can do to sharpen my A.I.M. (actionable, intentional, measurable) are:

_____   _____   _____

_____   _____   _____

Medicine

It has been said before that, "Every drug has a side effect." It doesn't matter if it is cocaine, coffee, or ibuprofen. Every foreign substance that enters our bodies influences our internal systems, whether it is relieving pain, increasing muscular power, or inhibiting specific hormones. You need to be aware of this concept every time you think about taking any type of drug.

It has *also* been said that, "There are no such things as side effects, only effects." Wow. Now that we have established this, you are encouraged to understand YOUR health within the parameters of YOUR situation. Some of you reading this have medical histories, conditions, and situations that require certain medication. If you are under the care of a physician, and that is what has been prescribed, FOLLOW THE DOCTOR'S orders.

Anytime a drug is used, whether it is pharmaceutical, recreational, or otherwise, there are a cascade of neurochemical reactions that are taking place. Furthermore, depending on the potency, frequency, and duration of the intake of any drug, your body will be affected, in terms of its ability to heal, create an addiction, and/or alter your body's normal functioning.

The truth of the matter is that the human brain, with all of its command centers is mankind's original drug store. It creates, releases, and transmits the necessary hormones that we need for optimal functioning. When an individual abuses drugs, they are in essence swaying the neurochemical functioning of their bodies.

Think of it this way, a vehicle has various containers for different fluids: oil, windshield wiper fluid, gasoline, power steering fluid, brake fluid, etc. If you run too low, or run out, your vehicle won't function at its best. Even worse, if you have too much of any of these fluids in any respective container, you will run into serious problems as well. It gets even worse: If you put oil in the gasoline tank, or windshield wiper fluid where the power steering is supposed to go, the outcome could put you in serious danger. This is metaphorically what happens to us when we abuse or misuse drugs.

I currently grade myself (1-5…1 is terrible, 5 is excellent): _____

My desired grade is: _____

Some things I can do to sharpen my A.I.M. (actionable, intentional, measurable) are:

_____ _____ _____

_____ _____ _____

Massage

Massage is a critical part of recovery. Our tissues, muscles, bones, and ligaments are under duress during training, preparation, and performance. When you start talking about muscles more specifically, it is very important for the muscles to be able to rebound and recover in a healthy manner.

Massage is great for recovery because not only does it change the muscle tone, but it helps get rid of toxins and any inflammation or swelling as well. Massage also promotes blood flow. As an athlete, blood is of utmost importance to you. It provides vital nutrients, and it's also good for healing.

Many professional athletes understand the importance of massage and have made it a part of their daily routine. Our muscles undergo so much tension that many athletes actually cannot differentiate between a tense muscle and a relaxed muscle (please see the section on progressive muscle relaxation). Getting a massage is the equivalent of having a healthy reset button. If the muscle is always under tension and it is not given time to recover, not only are you in danger of having compromised performance, but you are in danger of injury.

There are many forms of massage, some of which are simple, others of which are highly complex and would require a trained professional. Although we will not be getting into the intricacies of the different types of massage in this book, one that you should look to for regular consideration is self-myofascial release. This is typically when you use an implement such as a foam roller, a lacrosse ball, or some other type of external object in which you roll over a desired muscle group. This is done as the name implies, by yourself.

Other types of massages to look into are deep tissue massage, performance massage, lymphatic, and trigger point massage. Again, one of the primary benefits of massage is that it promotes the circulation of blood, which promotes healing and helps to reset your muscles for future performance.

I currently grade myself (1-5…1 is terrible, 5 is excellent): _____

My desired grade is: _____

Some things I can do to sharpen my A.I.M. (actionable, intentional, measurable) are:

_____   _____   _____

_____   _____   _____

Genetic IQ

Quite simply, everyone must attempt to know their family's health history. You do not have to have a doctoral level understanding, but you should be familiar with any ailments or conditions that run in your family. Some families are very open with each other about this type of information, whereas there are other families that are tight-lipped and secretive. Regardless of where your family lies on the spectrum, for your sake and those you love, it is imperative that you have a base level understanding of this information. There are many benefits, most importantly, the fact that it will allow you to get ahead of anything that you may be predisposed to. It will also help you plan for your health and the health of those you love.

The sad reality is that many people do not want to understand their family's health history. One of the reasons is for fear that they, their children, or significant other may be at risk to certain types of diseases. At times, it is used as a protective measure to keep information away from family members. Regardless of what may or may not be happening behind the scenes, it is your responsibility to research and ask questions.

Collecting family health history may not be easy, as some common barriers include, but are not limited to, distance (how far you live geographically from members of your family), culture/cultural norms, gender (mothers, grandmothers, and other female members of one's family may be more prone to share information than male counterparts), and motivation to actually be diligent in the collection of the information.

A knowledge of your family's health history has been shown in research to aid in management, diagnosis, and prevention of many chronic diseases and disorders, more specifically cardiovascular occurrences, diabetes, and certain types of cancers. Keep in mind that you may not be able to capture the complete picture of your family's health history. It is not an exact science by any means. As a matter of fact, studies show that it is not uncommon for key pieces of information to be missing. The most important thing is to be diligent and proactive.

I currently grade myself (1-5…1 is terrible, 5 is excellent): _____

My desired grade is: _____

Some things I can do to sharpen my A.I.M. (actionable, intentional, measurable) are:

_____   _____   _____

_____   _____   _____

Deep Breathing

Diaphragmatic breathing is one of the simplest, yet most powerful things you can do to improve your health and well-being. The research and the benefits are vast, and breathing from your diaphragm has a positive effect on your heart rate, stress levels, blood pressure, cognition, and various other workings of your body. As an athlete, your breathing acts as a proverbial brake, accelerator, and steering wheel during any type of performance. Even for simple brain performance, your brain requires oxygen and glucose to perform at high levels. Flooding your system with oxygen with even a few intentional minutes of deep breathing will work wonders for your well-being.

Your mother, father, or grandparents probably gave you some simple advice when you were young and in the midst of throwing a tantrum. They probably told you to slow down and take a deep breath. That information was not only practical, but it was also rooted in science. When you take into consideration the brain's feeding pattern, one of the last areas to receive these critical nutrients (oxygen, glucose, and others) is the frontal lobe. Why is that important? The frontal lobe is where higher order thinking takes place, strategic thinking, innovation, problem-solving, and other important brain activity. If this area is not saturated with ample levels of oxygen, it is difficult (if not impossible), to be able to think, let alone perform at high levels for extended periods of time.

Dr. Viktor Frankl, author of the internationally acclaimed book, *Man's Search For Meaning*, witnessed many of the catastrophic events that took place in Auschwitz during the egregious times of Nazi reign. He was famous for stating, *"Between stimulus and response, there is a space. In that space is our ability to choose, and in our choice lies growth and freedom."* This is powerful and relevant because many times the proverbial space that we need lies in our breathing. How many times do we get cut off in traffic, does somebody say something to us, are we offended, or umpires and officials make horrible game-altering calls, are we cheated, etc.? In most of those cases, our immediate recourse after that 'stimulus' is revenge/retaliation. The problem with immediately reacting after every stimulus is that we become knee-jerk reactors in our approach to life, which in turn, has a negative effect on our performance while we are competing. Taking the appropriate time to breathe and create space shifts us from being reactors to responders.

When you hear the term 'responder,' what comes to mind?

For many people, they think of *first responders*: paramedics, EMTs, police, fire fighters, nurses, athletic trainers, etc., as those who provide aid in a chaotic situation. These individuals are typically the calmest people in the room. They are able to access their higher order thinking because their breathing is likely under control. They know who needs care first and who can wait. They are trained to maintain their cool and keep their heads, while others may be losing theirs, so to speak.

When chaos and drama ensue, are you in control of your breathing? Are you a reactor? Or, are you more of a responder?

I currently grade myself (1-5…1 is terrible, 5 is excellent): _____

My desired grade is: _____

Some things I can do to sharpen my A.I.M. (actionable, intentional, measurable) are:

_____   _____   _____

_____   _____   _____

Exercise

When it comes to filling your buckets, exercise is one of the areas that you get the highest return on investment. Having a regular exercise routine positively affects your entire body. From your respiratory system, central nervous system, to even your lymphatic system, exercise is king.

Healthily stressing and training your body's complex system of bones, joints, and muscles prepares it to emerge even stronger. Anytime an organism is stressed, there is some type of inherent response. If you stress it too much, you induce damage (or worse); however, if you stress it too little, not much happens. Stressed just right (eustress), you induce growth. Healthy things grow. Healthy people grow as well.

This is especially true for athletes. Athletes, unlike other people, are regularly required to perform at high levels. These high levels include not only the use of creativity and intelligence, but physical prowess and athleticism. Exercise, the systematic subjection to stress, is one of the easiest and best ways for your body to reach new performance levels.

The reason why this is important is because when introduced at the appropriate time, exercise can propel an athlete's development. The inverse is true as well. Irreverent and careless exercise can be detrimental and set an athlete backward.

Exercise is not only great for the athlete as it relates to development and upcoming performances, it is tremendous as a source of recovery as well. Many athletes who are stressed, and those who have not worked out or trained in a long period of time, report exercise as a form of "reset" and recovery. The benefits are massive.

Exercise is also a litmus test for your levels of readiness. Exercise is a requirement for growth. You cannot have one without the other.

I currently grade myself (1-5…1 is terrible, 5 is excellent): _____

My desired grade is: _____

Some things I can do to sharpen my A.I.M. (actionable, intentional, measurable) are:

_____   _____   _____

_____   _____   _____

Progressive Muscle Relaxation

As stated earlier in the massage section, many athletes cannot tell the difference between a tense muscle and a relaxed muscle. We constantly walk around in a state of tension. Our traps, hamstrings, hips, and lower back are tight, and on down the line. One of the best methods to help muscles not only relax, but to gain a sense of self-awareness, is progressive muscle relaxation.

Progressive muscle relaxation occurs when an athlete first scans their body for any areas of tightness, pain or discomfort, and they proceed to contract that muscle group such as the hamstrings, traps, forearms, et cetera, for anywhere between three to five seconds.

They release the contraction and proceed to repeat this process throughout the entire body. After this process has occurred, the athlete will then take inventory in terms of perceived tightness, discomfort, et cetera, and typically, what will happen is that the athlete will enter a more relaxed state.

This is one of the most powerful techniques to help a muscle relax, particularly after a rough performance, leading into a performance, or simply as a means of recovery. The benefits are tremendous, and if anything, it helps an athlete with self-awareness within his or her body. Furthermore, not only can progressive muscle relaxation be used 'pre' and 'post' competition, athletes can use these techniques *within* their performances as well. Some research has highlighted the fact that progressive muscle relaxation training improves cognitive performance.

Progressive muscle relaxation is powerful and may provide immediate relief. One of the reasons this is so is because not only are higher order areas, such as the cerebral cortex and cerebellum activated, but the actual muscles that are tensed are sending messages to your brainstem and spinal cord as well. This then stimulates both a 'top-down' and 'bottom-up' effect.

Progressive muscle relaxation has shown to be a stalwart when it comes to reducing physical and cognitive stress, anxiety, and proves to be an important tool for athletes to possess.

I currently grade myself (1-5…1 is terrible, 5 is excellent): _____

My desired grade is: _____

Some things I can do to sharpen my A.I.M. (actionable, intentional, measurable) are:

_____   _____   _____

_____   _____   _____

Nutrition

It is likely that growing up, most of us heard that *inputs affect outputs*. The same can be said for your nutrition. Good diet and nutrition aids in improving your overall function and physical state. The quality of food and drink that you put into your body affects the availability of certain nutrients and ultimately the performance that occurs on the field.

Since this book is written for athletes, we would be remiss if we did not mention the analogy that you've likely heard before: high-end supercars, such as Ferrari, Lamborghini, et cetera, only take premium fuel.

As a matter of fact, it doesn't even have to be a super car. It can be a regular car that you buy at an everyday dealership. There are different grades of fuel for a reason. The higher the level of fuel, the higher the quality. The higher the quality, the higher the longevity of the engine, resulting in higher performance.

The same can be said for you as an athlete. If you choose to put in high grade nutrients into your diet, your performance, your recovery, and your overall health and wellbeing will benefit. The inverse of this is true as well. If you are taking in low grade food, junk food, processed food, food that has been stripped of all nutritional qualities and is just a quick fix to hunger, your health and wellbeing, recovery, and ultimately performance will suffer. There is no getting around it; this is a fact. It should also come as no surprise that increases in body fat has also been shown to decrease performance.

Nutrition is paramount, and it is a good idea for you to join forces with a nutritionist, a registered dietician, or a respected food expert, health and fitness coach, and the like, to augment this portion of your career. Everyone is looking for an edge, and those who excel in this area may outlast their peers.

If you haven't noticed, food is well over a multi-billion dollar industry, and there are many forces that are fighting for your dollars and your attention to sell you their food. While the cost of good food is going up, 'convenient' foods continue to abound all around us. When it comes to your nutrition, make sure you are taking advantage of the information that is out there. Self-education is typically regarded as the primary source of information about sports nutrition.

Not only should you have a solid grasp of your nutrient intake, but nutritional supplementation (i.e. protein shakes, recovery aids, etc) as well. Educate yourself, do not live in ignorance, and take control of your nutrition.

I currently grade myself (1-5…1 is terrible, 5 is excellent): _____

My desired grade is: _____

Some things I can do to sharpen my A.I.M. (actionable, intentional, measurable) are:

_____   _____   _____

_____   _____   _____

Hydration

Hydration is very similar to what you just read regarding nutrition. Water is one of the most important elements for both performance, and in the maintenance of life itself. Whether you're talking about a plant or a human being, water is not only important, it is necessary.

The majority of our bodies, 60% or so, are comprised of water. Our brains are composed of about 80% water. Therefore, if we are not doing our part in being intentional, all of our functioning, whether that's running, jumping, hitting, kicking, punching, et cetera, will be compromised. Water allows our organs to function more smoothly. It allows digestion to occur more soundly. It provides our muscles' elasticity, and it serves a host of other functions.

Although water is consumed directly as a beverage, many athletes consume water by way of the foods they eat (i.e. fruits, vegetables, etc.). Directly hydrating with water, however, is of utmost importance because athletes can lose up to 5% or more of their body weight during the course of an athletic competition. If an athlete is not properly hydrated, research has shown that as little as 2% dehydration can lead to detrimental effects on the field.

Timing of athlete hydration is important. Since many athletes are not voluntarily or adequately hydrated during competition, it is not uncommon to feel the effects of dehydration well after a competition. Simply put, it is critical that you hydrate not only before competition, but well after so that you do not unknowingly stay in a dehydrated state.

Dehydration leads directly into the conversation about cognitive performance. It is well studied in literature that dehydration has an adverse effect on your ability to use your mental faculties. Mild dehydration can impact things such as mood, concentration, and even short-term memory. However, more intense dehydration can have a negative impact on gastrointestinal function, heart function, kidney function, and can lead to the development of certain types of headaches.

As an athlete, you should keep in mind that physical work increases heat production within your body. Being properly hydrated is essential to dissipate heat. If you fail to replace fluid, it compromises the ability of your circulatory system to simultaneously maintain sufficient blood flow to both your skin and your muscles. This leads to muscle fatigue and an increase in body temperature. So if you live or work out in a warmer climate, hydration is even *more* critical.

This list might seem concerning, but do not be alarmed. Just be proactive and diligent when it comes to creating a hydrated environment within your body!

I currently grade myself (1-5...1 is terrible, 5 is excellent): _____

My desired grade is: _____

Some things I can do to sharpen my A.I.M. (actionable, intentional, measurable) are:

_____ _____ _____

_____ _____ _____

Key Terms:

- Exercise
- Progressive Muscle Relaxation
- Nutrition
- Hydration
- Sleep
- Medicine
- Massage
- Self-Myofacial Release
- Genetic IQ

Study Questions:

1. Which of the following techniques assist in scanning the body for tension and entering a more relaxed state?
   a. Progressive Muscle Relaxation
   b. Massage
   c. PETTLEP Model
   d. Mindfulness

2. True or False: Our bodies and brains are only slightly composed of water.

3. Which of the following functions affect nearly all human functions?
   a. Yearly Doctor's Visits
   b. Breakfast
   c. Perfectionism
   d. Sleep

4. True or False: Massage has the potential of changing muscle tone, aids in removing waste, and aids in blood circulation.

Part II

Psychological

After reading this section, you should be able to:

- ✓ explain why laughter is a powerful recovery aid

- ✓ describe the importance of play and human recovery

- ✓ list several means whereby an athlete can psychologically reset

- ✓ identify how different activities positively affect human psychology

Reading

As athletes work out and train their muscles to perform physically, it is important that you train your mind so it can perform mentally. Reading is one of the most powerful exercises you can participate in for mental engagement and recovery. Reading forces you to retrieve information, mentally paint pictures, innovate, comprehend, and connect. When you read, you are requiring yourself to make several mental connections with what you know, what you have learned in the past, and what you can do in the future. Reading and learning abilities are highly connected, as there are also many metacognitive skills that are related to reading.

Many people may turn on a movie or listen to music. However, reading engages your brain in a unique way in which you are connecting ideas to activities and painting vivid mental pictures. Reading is also one of the activities that brings you the biggest return on your investment, because you are able to take decades of experience from the author and consume it in hours.

Reading also builds on top of all prior knowledge. When you read, you are able to make neuronal connections with everything that you have amassed in your mental toolbox beforehand. Why is this important? The reason this is of utmost importance is because some of the leading contributing psychologists have posited that one of the highest forms of peak performance, human potential, or self-actualization is *creativity*.

An athlete's ability to create in an upcoming performance, especially within competition, is directly related to his or her ability to connect to the fundamentals, prior forms of information, and training that they have stored. Reading is a sure-fire way to secure this.

To pour fuel on the proverbial fire, you should consider adding reflection, discussion and writing into your reading regimen because meaningful reading requires your brain to build connections that attach meanings to what you are absorbing.

Reading is both restorative and reflective. If you have not incorporated much reading into your daily routine, it is suggested that you do so because this is an amazing form of recovery.

I currently grade myself (1-5…1 is terrible, 5 is excellent): _____

My desired grade is: _____

Some things I can do to sharpen my A.I.M. (actionable, intentional, measurable) are:

_____   _____   _____

_____   _____   _____

Meditation

Meditation is an interesting construct within the realm of recovery. People use meditation for different reasons. Some use meditation to enter a more relaxed state *before* doing something intense, such as a playoff game, a tournament, et cetera. Others use meditation *after* they have just completed a serious event with high implications.

Some research has shown that *brief* meditation sessions may offer motivational benefits as it relates to personal goals. On the other hand, those who engage in *high* levels of meditation have been seen to have high levels of self-compassion and happiness. Research is rich in instances whereby regular practices of meditation have been shown to promote positive psychological effects, well-being, and emotional balance.

There are other individuals who incorporate meditation as part of their regular routine, just as they lift weights, run, and train. They also meditate as part of keeping with their personal equilibrium as a spiritual practice. Some individuals use meditation with their prayer or any type of faith practices. When you look at the seminal roots of the of the word *meditation*, it is a constant dwelling upon, mulling, contemplation, or reflection. It's a regurgitation and concentrated focus on concepts, constructs, and teachings.

As human beings, we have one stomach that's responsible for all of our digestion and food intake. When you study a cow, however, it has four stomachs. The word meditation comes from the concept of regurgitation. When a cow eats food, it will chew the food, and regurgitate it. Then, it'll continue to chew incessantly. This process continues, and is cyclical in nature.

The word 'meditate' means a constant dwelling upon something. So when you're meditating on a concept, a thought, a scripture, a teaching point, or whatever the case may be, it means that you're dwelling upon something that you are actively trying to get into your spirit and mind.

For some people, meditation is far less complex. There is more of a 'letting go' than anything else. Being present and self-aware becomes the focus. Some forms of mindfulness meditation, for example, heightens self-awareness, acknowledges thoughts, and lets them pass non-judgementally.

So whatever it is that you use meditation for, it can be a powerful tool in your toolbox because it allows your mind to review, renew, and to rest.

I currently grade myself (1-5…1 is terrible, 5 is excellent): _____

My desired grade is: _____

Some things I can do to sharpen my A.I.M. (actionable, intentional, measurable) are:

_____   _____   _____

_____   _____   _____

Prayer

Many people believe in a power or a source higher than themselves, and prayer is a regular part of their lives. It is a consistent part of their routine. It is a regular part of connecting with someone greater than themselves. As research has shown, prayer has serious implications on well-being. Some studies indicate that prayer has been shown to promote recovery and healing when used in conjunction with medical care.

There is even research to suggest that certain types of prayer, such as prayers of thanksgiving, are significant predictors of positive well-being.

If you are an individual who prays, and that's part of your routine and your process, you are encouraged to continue to do so. Prayer has been shown to have profound effects on not only our performance but our perspectives. Prayer and spirituality within the medical field has yielded some great findings in terms of their benefits.

When you break prayer down to its basic constituents, you will typically find hope and expectancy, which by themselves are prime movers in science when you study motivation. When you come across individuals who pray, you typically find that they are people who believe in something or someone bigger than themselves.

Research has shown that prayer, as an intervention, can help patients achieve relaxation, rest, well-being, and peace. Furthermore, in some instances in the health profession, prayer is recognized as a complementary alternative treatment, and part of a more holistic approach for patient care.

Prayer also has a calming effect in reducing anxiety, and it acts as a release for many players in times of cognitive stress and pressure-packed moments in an athlete's life.

I currently grade myself (1-5…1 is terrible, 5 is excellent): _____

My desired grade is: _____

Some things I can do to sharpen my A.I.M. (actionable, intentional, measurable) are:

_____   _____   _____

_____   _____   _____

Journaling

Journaling is a big part of many athletes' careers, and it is an important part when it comes to mental recovery. Journaling is the kinesthetic version of reflection. When you journal, you are, in essence, unloading volumes of information, thoughts, reactions, and observations onto paper. Journaling has been shown to lower rumination and anxiety.

Journaling has many benefits including: encouraging creativity, improving self-awareness, promoting self-organization, increasing centeredness, and has a positive impact on the immune system. Many people who journal have expressed a proverbial load being lifted off of their shoulders.

There are also several different types of journaling. Ironically, regardless of how messy or disorganized your journaling approach may be, it can be highly liberating.

The average human being has tens of thousands of thoughts every single day. What do you think would happen if there was no healthy place to reflect on these thoughts? Have you ever thought of what would happen if you could not talk to someone? How about if you were in a foreign country (as many professionals are) and could not effectively verbalize or communicate how you were feeling with a family member or close friend?

Journaling allows you to freely express yourself through pen and paper (or for some digitally) in a manner in which you can direct your thoughts in a constructive manner.

Many athletes, unfortunately, do not have someone to healthily share thoughts with, and when they do not journal, at times the thoughts have nowhere to go and the thoughts swirl around in their heads. The problem with this, however, is that at some point these unattended thoughts, feelings, and concerns will express themselves in the form of withdrawal, an outburst, or the athlete may just shut down.

I currently grade myself (1-5...1 is terrible, 5 is excellent): _____

My desired grade is: _____

Some things I can do to sharpen my A.I.M. (actionable, intentional, measurable) are:

_____   _____   _____

_____   _____   _____

Music

Music is an important part of many athletes' careers. Music is one of the easiest ways to change an environment. It's interesting because when you go into a professional or collegiate weight room, one of the things that all athletes argue over is whose music they're going to listen to! Music is very personal, and carries deep meaning, for many athletes.

In certain situations, music can be used to heighten intensity, while in others, music can be used to literally put people to sleep. Without getting into the hard science of brainwaves, the pitch, tone, bpm, and rhythm, understand this: music can directly impact physiological and psychological functioning. Music is one of the simplest ways to aid in recovery, change an environment, or to positively influence one's mental state.

Music has tremendous effects on those who play it, those who compose it, and those who simply listen to it. One of the reasons this is true is because music has the ability to activate the emotional and reward networks of the brain.

As an athlete, music is a powerful source of nostalgia: a wishful longing for the past, especially those that conjure up pleasant emotions. Music that was played during your formative years (your youth) and during critical moments likely impacted your future mindsets and environments. This is important because nostalgia has the potential to not only impact motivation, but to inhibit negative and unpleasant stimuli.

Music's impact on a performance or career can be as simple as changing a mood, or as complex as engaging in music therapy. Music therapy can mediate factors involving cognition, conduct, concentration, and even impact movement patterns. It is also important to pay attention to the lyrics in your music of choice as well. The words and lyrics we repeat and allow in our minds are just as impactful, if not more so, than the instruments and beats over which they are performed.

I currently grade myself (1-5...1 is terrible, 5 is excellent): _____

My desired grade is: _____

Some things I can do to sharpen my A.I.M. (actionable, intentional, measurable) are:

_____   _____   _____

_____   _____   _____

Laughter

Laughter is a tremendous way to recover after an intense game, tournament, or practice session. When one is engaged in laughter, endorphins are released, oxytocin is affected, and general health and wellbeing are improved. It is not uncommon to see several high-level athletes engage in laughter, especially in critical in-game scenarios. They will engage in cracking jokes by using sarcasm, wittiness, and the like.

To ease the tension in high-stakes environments, some athletes watch hours of comedy shows before competition. This is interesting because it perfectly illustrates the concept of relentless recovery. Laughter has been shown, in research, to have positive psychological and physiological effects. Not only is laughter one of the integral factors of happiness and contentment, research is showing that the absence of laughter may lead to pathology and dysfunctional behavior.

Remember, the opposite of relentless recovery is burnout. There are several ways that you can engage in this stress relieving activity. You can go to a comedy show, watch funny movies, or hang out with quick-witted friends. Research has shown that laughter after watching humorous movies may lead to a decrease of certain stress hormones.

Furthermore, the neurobiological benefits of laughter have been shown to include relaxed muscle tone, decreased anxiety, and increased beta-endorphins. Laughter can make heavy demands on your brain, but the results may be worth it.

Laughter also draws us closer together, and has been shown to have several benefits amongst individuals, especially those people you work with, compete with, and share life with. Research also suggests that those with the greatest sense of humor typically exhibit lower levels of anticipatory anxiety. As you can see, laughter is a tremendous way to engage in recovery.

I currently grade myself (1-5…1 is terrible, 5 is excellent): _____

My desired grade is: _____

Some things I can do to sharpen my A.I.M. (actionable, intentional, measurable) are:

_____   _____   _____

_____   _____   _____

Entertainment

It goes without saying that one of the ways in which we can help our bodies and minds recover is to engage in something fun and refreshing *other* than our performance. Entertainment comes in all forms, and it has an interesting way of taking our minds off of stress…at least temporarily. Some forms of entertainment can be detrimental and negatively addictive, while other forms of entertainment should be encouraged.

Many athletes use other sports as their entertainment. For instance, many athletes love to golf. Some athletes engage in board games, card games, or they go see shows, movies, etc. Others spend time at theatre performances and plays with their family members and friends. They go fishing and hunting, amongst many other activities. The key is to find something that is healthy, that will edify you in between practices, competition, and training.

Entertainment is a great way to aid in recovery. You have probably recognized that there are some similarities between some of these categories. Entertainment is a bucket where many of the recovery methods listed in this book can be taken from. For instance, entertainment and hobbies seem alike. While they are, there are some distinct differences. Entertainment is broad; it is a general well from which to draw. Hobbies are specific (i.e. dancing, biking, shooting, etc). Similarly, recovery aids like music and laughter can come from the entertainment bucket.

The end-goal of entertainment is to provide the end-user (you) amusement or enjoyment. Entertainment can be as extensive as going to the SuperBowl or attending an epic Broadway production in New York. It can be as simple as building paper airplanes with your nieces or nephews, or watching street performers at Venice Beach. Either way, that end-goal of entertainment is to provide amusement or enjoyment, which are critical for accelerating your recovery from the rigors of competition and training.

I currently grade myself (1-5...1 is terrible, 5 is excellent): _____

My desired grade is: _____

Some things I can do to sharpen my A.I.M. (actionable, intentional, measurable) are:

_____ _____ _____

_____ _____ _____

Play

Play is an important part of recovery. Whether an athlete has been injured, is experiencing the rigors of a competitive season, or going through a tough time, it is very important that he or she embraces the concept of play. Dr. Stuart Brown has contributed tremendously in this area and has listed eight different types of play in his book, *Play*. It is ironic that we're talking about play, being that the target audience of this book is athletes, who 'play' for a living. It is vital to understand what play is and what it can do.

When you are playing, you're arguably not working. When you are playing, you're likely not stressing. When you're playing, anxiety seemingly dissipates. When you're playing, you're having fun. This type of fun aids in recovery.

Play conjures up emotions of joy, competition, expectancy, rewards, and camaraderie. This cocktail of emotions has positive impacts on one's health and wellbeing.

There are several categories of play that can have positive psychological benefits. Even video game play has been shown to positively impact cognitive abilities. FMRI scans have even, on occasion, been shown to register higher brain activity in children who played video games for several hours in regions of the human brain associated with attention, impulse control and working memory when compared to their peers who didn't play.

When you see individuals playing, it may be difficult to find someone among them who is sad, lethargic, hopeless, or disconnected.

Play brings people together, and helps to elevate the morale of any environment. This is even true within the animal kingdom. Play is where young lions learn the essential skills of hunting. They test their strength and come to understand hierarchy and order. Play provides temporary respite from the outside world.

If you are experiencing burnout, find an area in which you can engage in play and watch how quickly you begin to accelerate your recovery process.

I currently grade myself (1-5…1 is terrible, 5 is excellent): _____

My desired grade is: _____

Some things I can do to sharpen my A.I.M. (actionable, intentional, measurable) are:

_____   _____   _____

_____   _____   _____

Hobbies

There is an inherent difference between play and hobbies, but the two are very similar. A hobby is any activity that you regularly engage in for pleasure during your free time. People engage in different hobbies for different reasons.

Hobbies can be calm and relaxing, such as gardening, hiking, or sculpting. They can also be much more physically charged and engaging. Hobbies can include creative, athletic, and intellectual activities. Either way, hobbies have been shown to help reduce stress.

Hobbies can also be a form of play. It is ironic, but when we are under the most stress and life seems toughest, we forget to engage in these creative parts of our lives. We forget about our hobbies, but these hobbies bring balance to our lives just as much as our work brings value to our lives.

Hobbies are a form of release; they help us express ourselves creatively. Hobbies are outlets which we can use to take energy, innovation, and even stress and channel them into something productive, or to simply pass time. Think of hobbies as vehicles in which you can creatively take ideas or energy that you have and transform them into a novel accomplishment or an epic creation.

Engaging in hobbies is one of the most simple and time-tested ways for someone to hit the reset button. Nearly everyone has some type of hobby. From the president of a growing nation to a prisoner who is in the middle of a life sentence, almost everyone engages in a hobby.

I currently grade myself (1-5…1 is terrible, 5 is excellent): _____

My desired grade is: _____

Some things I can do to sharpen my A.I.M. (actionable, intentional, measurable) are:

_____ _____ _____

_____ _____ _____

Key Terms:

> ➢ Meditation
> ➢ Prayer
> ➢ Journaling
> ➢ Reading
> ➢ Music
> ➢ Laughter
> ➢ Entertainment
> ➢ Play
> ➢ Hobbies

Study Questions:

1. What is considered the kinesthetic version of reflection and can aid in reducing rumination?
   a. Affirmations
   b. Focus
   c. Proactive Visualization
   d. Journaling

2. True or False: Reading assists in creating neuronal connections

3. Which of the following ways can quickly aid in reducing cognitive anxiety?
   a. Coffee & Donuts
   b. Prayer & Meditation
   c. Jumping & Olympic Power Cleans
   d. Family Time & Nutrition

4. True or False: Listening to music, attending a comedy show, or playing board games can be an effective means of psychological recovery.

Part III

Environmental

After reading this section, you should be able to:

- ✓ describe how one's environment aids in recovery

- ✓ recommend various ways to improve both social & physical environments

- ✓ evaluate if an environment is healthy & conducive for recovery

- ✓ improve upon any existing environments that may be problematic

Décor

Did you know that the color of your walls can influence your mood, behavior, and feelings? What do Chick-fil-A, McDonald's, In-N-Out Burger, and Sonic all have in common? Yes, you guessed it: their colors. Red, white, or yellow are their primary colors. Those colors have been shown to be some of the most highly converting colors. When it comes to fast-food restaurants, people don't typically go there and hang out for hours on end. The furniture in fast-food restaurants is not necessarily comfortable, and neither is the paint.

If the interior of your house is painted red, it may spur heightened feelings of intensity or aggression, without you even knowing it. If the inside of your room is painted in a very light blue, it has a tendency to do the opposite. Colors matter. Décor matters. If you have plants inside of your home, especially live plants, research has shown that stress and anxiety levels go down. The décor and the way that your home is designed matters.

Our brains see every item within our living spaces as pieces of information. The lamp is a piece of information, the countertops, the floors, furniture, paintings, trash, etc. are all pieces of information. The more organized, clean, and thoughtful these pieces of information are presented, the more calming effect it has on one's mind. The inverse of this is true also. If there is clutter lying about in an untidy room, your brain bounces back-and-forth, and for some people it causes mental chaos.

Things such as plants, well placed mirrors, intentional lighting, etc. can totally transform a room, thus making it a more welcoming environment for recovery and rejuvenation.

You do not have to have a crazy budget to remodel your living space; you just need to be intentional. There are plenty of resources available to help you think through an endless amount of possibilities. Your décor can consciously and subconsciously help you enter into a state of recovery.

I currently grade myself (1-5…1 is terrible, 5 is excellent): _____

My desired grade is: _____

Some things I can do to sharpen my A.I.M. (actionable, intentional, measurable) are:

_____   _____   _____

_____   _____   _____

Sunlight

Exposure to sunlight has serious health and recovery implications. Our circadian rhythms, biological processes, and moods are all affected by sunlight. It is a known fact that regions that are overcast, or do not have continual access to the sun, report higher feelings of anxiety and lower mood. Exposure to sunlight is also necessary for the healthy production of Vitamin D.

Our exposure to sunlight actually affects our ability to sleep in the upcoming days. Sunlight affects digestive patterns and several biological processes that are important. When people are exposed to sunlight in the morning, the natural melatonin production happens much sooner (and more efficiently), which means you may enter into sleep more easily at night. When talking about the recovery process, sunlight is extremely important.

Certain psychological disorders are actually associated with one's inability to have access to proper sunlight. There are certain regions in the world that are bereft of adequate sunlight. As a result, the moods, emotions, and feelings of those who live in those environments are negatively affected.

At a cellular level, sunlight is a prime mover of several biological processes. When we take a look at the biopsychosocial model, sunlight is actually an area that affects all three (biology, psychology, and environment). The sun's rays help to increase your levels of endorphins and serotonin. Why is this important? Because all of these chemical messengers: melatonin, endorphins, and serotonin can DIRECTLY impact your ability to perform.

So how much is enough? You should talk to your physician, and take into consideration things such as age, occupation, lifestyle, where you live geographically, and other factors. Healthy sun intake, the use of appropriate hats, sunscreen, and exposure avoidance where possible, are appropriate strategies to help mitigate risk.

Although you do not need to incessantly sunbathe or spend inordinate amounts of time in the sun, be mindful that a proper relationship with the sun and your biological rhythms are having a direct impact on your ability to not only perform, but to recover.

I currently grade myself (1-5…1 is terrible, 5 is excellent): _____

My desired grade is: _____

Some things I can do to sharpen my A.I.M. (actionable, intentional, measurable) are:

_____ _____ _____

_____ _____ _____

Nature

Similar to the sun's impact on our performance, our exposure to nature is important in helping us reset our minds as well. Nature includes anything from sunlight to trees, water, mountains, grass, and the like. Research has shown that when we are exposed to nature, it has a positive effect on our health and well-being. Our interaction with nature has been shown to increase self-esteem, lead to feelings of renewal, and a decrease in stress.

Those of us who live in the city should be encouraged to get out of town as much as possible, and to expose ourselves to the ocean, mountains, and nature in general. Nature has the biophysical ability to reduce health risks. Some research has even indicated nature is a link to reduced all-cause mortality, reduced asthma, and general enhanced health.

Sometimes, we can't get out of town. However, going to our backyard, a local park, or finding contact with the earth's natural surface (i.e. sand, grass, etc.) has been shown to positively affect the electrical charge within our bodies.

Fractals, which are commonly seen in nature, have been shown to aid in health and well-being. Fractals are seemingly infinite patterns that are geometric, complex, and similar in nature. You can see fractals in trees, plants, water, pine cones, crystals, etc. For some reason, human beings enjoy viewing fractals in nature, and their effects are well documented.

Elements such as vegetation cover, and even the presence of birds in the environment have been linked to lower prevalence of depression, anxiety, and stress. Nature serves as an easy access point for athletes worldwide to hit the reset button. Something as simple as going on a walk, and experiencing fresh air and trees can have a profound effect on your health and wellbeing.

I currently grade myself (1-5…1 is terrible, 5 is excellent): _____

My desired grade is: _____

Some things I can do to sharpen my A.I.M. (actionable, intentional, measurable) are:

_____   _____   _____

_____   _____   _____

Quiet Zones

In our ever-bustling world, athletes find themselves connected more than ever. We are connected through technology more than any other time in human history. We have notifications and ringtones for everything imaginable. As our world grows, we also find ourselves with less and less privacy. Having a quiet place within our home, the locker room, our workplace, or anywhere else, is important for our health, well-being, and recovery.

People take sabbaticals for a reason. They take vacations for a reason. We go on retreats for a reason. The reality is that sometimes athletes cannot do that. Quiet zones are like mini-vacations and mini-escapes in which they can recharge before re-entering the fight. They have to be intentional about carving out time to energize themselves; it's necessary.

Having time alone to think, ponder, reflect, innovate, or problem-solve is a lost art in society. Some of the greatest revelations and insights are found when we are by ourselves, without technology. If you are in a situation where you can't seem to get away, you may have to be innovative with your alone time.

Quiet zones do not necessarily have to be within the borders of your house. They can be a well-thought-out area outside, on your porch, or in your backyard. It can also be a place away from your home, such as going on a walk, intentionally going to a park, or finding somewhere that many people are not frequenting so that you can enjoy quiet time. Quiet zones are important.

When constant noise is present, we tend to engage in adaptive strategies to block out noise; sometimes it can have an adverse effect on both our bodies and our minds.

Many professional athletes who are familiar with their respective stadiums/arenas and those of their opponents will often have predetermined quiet zones that they go to before a competition.

Quiet zones are great areas to pray, meditate, visualize, problem-solve, and just enjoy the silence away from any distraction. Contrary to popular opinion, sometimes we are able to solve problems by simply stepping away. Quiet zones allow our subconscious mind to go to work for us.

I currently grade myself (1-5…1 is terrible, 5 is excellent): _____

My desired grade is: _____

Some things I can do to sharpen my A.I.M. (actionable, intentional, measurable) are:

_____ _____ _____

_____ _____ _____

Family Time

Regardless of your family dynamic, where you were born, or where you were raised, family time is absolutely critical. All of our families have different structures and traditions, but one of the things that is universal, as it relates to human development, is our connectedness to our families. Having time to connect, share, listen, and engage our families is critical for our recovery.

Many athletes who are in a slump or struggling are revived quite quickly by a phone call, a video call, a text message, or a visit from a family member. In Maslow's hierarchy of needs, one of the key areas, as an individual progresses to self-actualization, is a sense of belonging. We, as human beings, inherently want to be loved, and we want to belong. When this is evident in our lives, it will aid in our recovery. It will aid in you hitting the reset button.

You may come from a family dynamic that is flawed. Guess what? We all do! No family is perfect. You may have animosity, unforgiveness, or bad blood among family members, but this is not uncommon. Despite it all, you are encouraged to forgive. As much as we need family time to help us, your family needs *you* to help them.

Family, in time, equates to connectedness, and when something is connected, it is stronger by definition. An individual horse or ox can pull thousands of pounds, but when horses and oxen are yoked together, it is not uncommon for them to pull an exponential amount together. Families can be the same way.

Remember, this dynamic works both ways. Not only should you be using family time to fill your proverbial tank, but you should be proactive in adding value and helping your family however and whenever you can.

I currently grade myself (1-5…1 is terrible, 5 is excellent): _____

My desired grade is: _____

Some things I can do to sharpen my A.I.M. (actionable, intentional, measurable) are:

_____ _____ _____

_____ _____ _____

Living Spaces

Much like the décor conversation, living spaces are also important. Where you live is critical to your ability to recover. To be clear, living spaces have nothing to do with what neighborhood you live in, or property values in your zip code. Living spaces have everything to do with how you are functioning within the space you call 'home'.

The biggest difference between décor and living spaces is décor has everything to do with the inanimate objects. For example, paint color, plants, design, room accessories, and feng shui (if you're into that) are examples of décor. Living spaces, on the other hand, have everything to do with the lively, animated people who go into those equations. These can be roommates, spouses, family members, et cetera.

Some of you reading this are in unhealthy living situations, and believe it or not, it is affecting your performance. You may need to consider changing your living situation so that this segment of your recovery equation is addressed.

Living spaces should be filled with people you can trust, people who are safe, and those who are adding to your life experience as an athlete. Unfortunately, sometimes living spaces are not necessarily chosen by us. At times, they can be mandated by the team, and we just have to deal with it. The hope lies in knowing that no living situation lasts forever. As an athlete, if you are ever in a situation where you are living with untrustworthy, unsafe, and chronically toxic individuals, you need to seek assistance leaving that situation immediately.

Remember, whatever you feed will grow. The longer you are in a toxic living situation, the more energy, effort, resources, and time you will spend living in and/or avoiding that situation. These same areas can be applied towards healthy living spaces, and can have a profoundly positive effect on your career as an athlete.

The people who are a part of your living spaces have the power to not only prevent you from a higher level of success, but they can propel you as well, when it comes to your ability to recover.

I currently grade myself (1-5…1 is terrible, 5 is excellent): _____

My desired grade is: _____

Some things I can do to sharpen my A.I.M. (actionable, intentional, measurable) are:

_____   _____   _____

_____   _____   _____

Safety

A wise man once said, "People run towards two things: they run towards love and they run towards safety." Whether that safety is psychological or physical, people will run towards that time and time again. It doesn't matter if you are a man, woman, child, young, or old, these things are inherent to the human experience.

People need safety, and they need certainty. If your environment, whether that's on the team, at home, or in your relationships are not safe, it may have a negative impact on your performance and your ability to bounce back and healthily recover. Again, when you look at Maslow's hierarchy of needs, this is a critical ingredient along the pathway to success. When you evaluate your environmental factors and feel safe in all of those places, it frees you up to perform physically and mentally.

When you evaluate the human brain, there are typically two things that your brain is trying to do: it wants to protect and it wants to predict.

Your brain wants to protect you from hurt, harm, and danger (whether this is physical or emotional). It is also trying to predict what is going to happen next. If any of these two areas are inhibited, your brain will feel threatened and your progress in any endeavor will be compromised.

Having safe relationships with people you can talk to about life, and your performance both on and off the field of competition is paramount. Having safe playing and living conditions is also key.

When there is safety, it frees you up to execute whatever your endeavors may be. Little children will usually be more at peace when they know their parents are present for their performances. A weightlifter may aim to lift more weight when he or she knows that there is a spotter to assist if needed. A sense of safety that is present in people, places, and things is key for relentless recovery.

I currently grade myself (1-5…1 is terrible, 5 is excellent): _____

My desired grade is: _____

Some things I can do to sharpen my A.I.M. (actionable, intentional, measurable) are:

_____   _____   _____

_____   _____   _____

Relationships

Human beings are complicated. Life is a web of relationships, and one relationship can affect several. Just as one good relationship can positively affect several, so can a bad one. It is very important when evaluating the relationships with our teammates, family members, coaches, and friends that we assess things that we have talked about thus far in this book.

It has been said that some individuals add to their relationships, while some take away, some multiply, and some divide. It is up to you to determine what people are doing in any relationship you find yourself in. We should, as much as possible, aim to live peaceably with all men and women.

There are some situations, unfortunately, whereby we are dealing with a toxic individual, and he or she is having an adverse effect on our ability to perform, as well as our ability to recover.

Here's the irony about toxicity: it only takes a little bit of that toxicity to corrupt the entire area, the entire person, or the entire relationship. As the old saying goes, "Show me your friends and I'll show you your future". There are also people who say that your projected future success can be determined by looking at the five people that you spend the most time with. Whatever metric that you use, there is a sliver of truth in all of these assertions. Our relationships with people need to continually be assessed. If any of those relationships are toxic, you cannot afford to maintain them. You must be willing to let them go.

To be clear, you cannot always cut off relationships and run away from bad situations. This isn't always possible. What you can control, however, is the energy, space, and attention you are giving these toxic people and situations. Remember, whatever you feed will grow. If you foster an environment for health, performance, and growth, the likelihood that you will be healthy, perform high, and grow will be high. The inverse of this is true as well. If you allow for an environment that welcomes toxicity, negativity, and mediocrity, these attributes will invade and ultimately destroy what you are trying to build.

Relationships matter. Healthy relationships have an overwhelmingly positive impact on your ability to recover on the court/field, and also in life.

I currently grade myself (1-5…1 is terrible, 5 is excellent): _____

My desired grade is: _____

Some things I can do to sharpen my A.I.M. (actionable, intentional, measurable) are:

_____ _____ _____

_____ _____ _____

Love

Love is an interesting thing. Many times when people hear the term 'love', it is romanticized, as in Hollywood, where there are undertones of it in nearly every movie or production. The definition of love that we will use here is *the sacrificial giving of oneself for the benefit of others*. When you love something or someone, you will give more time, energy, and attention to that thing or to that person. If you do not love someone or something, you will spend very little time, if any, with that person or thing.

Love will cause you to go the extra mile. Love will cause you to think of others. Love will cause you to become more selfless. Love will cause you to give. The ironic thing about love is that love almost always forces you to focus on other people. Even though this book is about you and your recovery, when you love people and are focused on them, ironically, you benefit from it as well. Truly loving and appreciating other people is one of the most selfless yet character-building activities that you can engage in. When you put all these things together, you have a great recipe for relentless recovery.

As a human being, when you feel loved, it puts you at ease. It allows you the mental and emotional capacity to get things done, because the environment is conducive to warmth and acceptance. Again, love is the sacrificial giving of oneself for the benefit of others. Love is one of the most reciprocal activities that you can engage in. Servant leadership, putting the team before yourself, thinking of how you can best help others, ultimately helps you and improves your mental and emotional well-being. It even has positive physiological effects as well.

Some models in psychology point to the fact that before you can be the highest and best version of yourself, you need love in the initial stages of human development. If you do not have an environment that is conducive to love, one can argue that it would be difficult, if not impossible, to reach the highest version of yourself.

The more you love, the more you give. The more you give, the more you get. Love is an integral part of relentless recovery.

I currently grade myself (1-5...1 is terrible, 5 is excellent): _____

My desired grade is: _____

Some things I can do to sharpen my A.I.M. (actionable, intentional, measurable) are:

_____   _____   _____

_____   _____   _____

Key Terms:

- ➤ Décor
- ➤ Sunlight
- ➤ Nature
- ➤ Quiet Zones
- ➤ Family Time
- ➤ Living Spaces
- ➤ Safety
- ➤ Relationships
- ➤ Love

Study Questions:

1. What element for the Environmental section deals largely with the inanimate dynamic of one's environment?
   a. Command Words
   b. Décor
   c. Arousal Regulation
   d. PMR

2. True or False: The construct of 'Safety' has both physical and psychological ramifications.

3. What has previously been defined as the sacrificial giving of oneself for the benefit of others?
   a. Relationships
   b. Perception
   c. Love
   d. Family Time

4. True or False: Exposure to sunlight can drastically affect a person's mood?

Now What? 80/20 Rule

You've gotten to the end of this book, and you may have several questions. That's okay. You have been given a lot of information, and some of the information you were absolutely clear on, and you may be questioning other areas.

You may have heard of the 80/20 rule, or what has been also known as Pareto's Principle. To simplify it in the most basic way, it suggests that 80% of the output in any given area is due to 20% of its inputs. Another way to say this is if you were to learn 10 amazing concepts, and start to apply them to your life, over the long-haul, only 20% (or 2 of these concepts) would yield the biggest return on investment. This principle has shown to be fairly reliable over the course of time, and in several industries.

So what does that mean for you? You have just been exposed to 27 areas whereby you can improve your potential when it comes to relentless recovery. According to the 80/20 Rule, there are going to be about 5 to 6 areas that are going to yield the biggest results for you along the way. This is not to indicate that paying attention to the other areas won't work; it's just reaffirming the fact that you are going to see SIGNIFICANT improvement because of this key 20%.

Your job now is to identify this 20% and begin to double down your efforts.

When you look at the following areas, how did you initially score? Now, circle those 5 or 6 areas in which you feel you are very good at, can do seamlessly, or you feel will positively impact your pursuit of relentless recovery:

____Sleep   ____Meds   ___Massage   ____Genetic IQ

____Deep Breathing   ____Exercise   ___PMR   ____Nutrition

____Reading   ____Meditation   ____Prayer   ____Journaling

____Music   ____Laughter   ____Entertainment   ____Play

____Hobbies   ____Family Time   ____Living Spaces   ____Safety

____Relationships ____Love   ____ Décor   ____Sunlight

____Nature   ___Quiet Zones   ____Hydration

Section I: Biological

Ansari, M., Hardcastle, S., Myers, S., & Williams, A. D. (2023). The Health and Functional Benefits of Eccentric versus Concentric Exercise Training: A Systematic Review and Meta-Analysis. Journal of Sports Science & Medicine, 22(2), 288–309.

Bajla, I., Holländer, I., Gmeiner, G., Reichel, C., & Holländer, I. (2005). Quantitative analysis of images in erythropoietin doping control. Medical & Biological Engineering & Computing, 43(3), 403–409.

Barry M Popkin, Kristen E D'Anci, Irwin H Rosenberg, Water, hydration, and health, Nutrition Reviews, Volume 68, Issue 8, 1 August 2010, Pages 439–458.

Cheah, K. J., & Cheah, L. J. (2023). Benefits and side effects of protein supplementation and exercise in sarcopenic obesity: A scoping review. Nutrition Journal, 22(1), 1–13.

Demirel, H. (2016). Sleep Quality Differs Between Athletes and Non-athletes. Clinical & Investigative Medicine, 39(6), S184–S186.

Haff, G., Triplett, N. (2016). Essentials of Strength and Conditioning 4th Edition. Human Kinetics.

Harada, T., Wada, K., Tsuji, F., Krejci, M., Kawada, T., Noji, T., Nakade, M., & Takeuchi, H. (2016). Intervention study using a leaflet entitled "three benefits of 'go to bed early! get up early! and intake nutritionally rich breakfast!' a message for athletes" to improve the soccer performance of university soccer team. Sleep & Biological Rhythms, 14, 65–74.

Ivy, J., Portman, R. (2004). Nutrient Timing. Basic Health Publications.

K. M. Keptner, C. Fitzgibbon, and J. O'Sullivan, "Effectiveness of anxiety reduction interventions on test anxiety: a comparison of four techniques incorporating sensory modulation," British Journal of Occupational Therapy, vol. 70, no. 6, pp. 1–9, 2020.

Kuang, K., & Gettings, P. E. (2020). Applying the theory of motivated information management to family health history. Personal Relationships, 27(4), 846–879.

Latona, V. (2000). Loosen up! Vegetarian Times, 273, 88.

Lei Xu, Jacobs, W., Odum, M., Melton, C., Holland, L., & Johnson, K. (2017). Are Young Adults Talking about Their Family Health History? A Qualitative Investigation. American Journal of Health Studies, 32(2), 60–69.

Liu, J. (2021). Relationship between Volleyball Sports Nutrition Food and Sports Athletes' Training and Physical Health Based on Medical Image Recognition. Computational & Mathematical Methods in Medicine, 1–13.

Loehr, J. (1994). The New Toughness Training For Sports: Mental, Emotional, and Physical Conditioning from One of the World's Premier Sports Psychologists. Plume.

Loren Toussaint, Quang Anh Nguyen, Claire Roettger, Kiara Dixon, Martin Offenbächer, Niko Kohls, Jameson Hirsch, Fuschia Sirois, "Effectiveness of Progressive Muscle Relaxation, Deep

Breathing, and Guided Imagery in Promoting Psychological and Physiological States of Relaxation", Evidence-Based Complementary and Alternative Medicine, vol. 2021, Article ID 5924040, 8 pages, 2021.

Magnolini, R., Falcato, L., Cremonesi, A., Schori, D., & Bruggmann, P. (2022). Fake anabolic androgenic steroids on the black market – a systematic review and meta-analysis on qualitative and quantitative analytical results found within the literature. BMC Public Health, 22(1), 1–15.

Mandic, G. F., Peric, M., Krzelj, L., Stankovic, S., & Zenic, N. (2013). Sports Nutrition and Doping Factors in Synchronized Swimming: Parallel Analysis among Athletes and Coaches. Journal of Sports Science & Medicine, 12(4), 753–760.

Moon, J. R. (2013). Body composition in athletes and sports nutrition: an examination of the bioimpedance analysis technique. European Journal of Clinical Nutrition, 67, S54–S59.

O'Brady, C. (2022). The 12 Hour Walk. Scribner.

Ostovar, A., Haerinejad, M. J., Akbarzadeh, S., & Keshavarz, M. (2017). Comparison of the Prevalence of Psychiatric Disorders in Performance-Enhancing Drug Users and Nonuser Bodybuilders. Iranian Journal of Psychiatry, 12(4), 220–225.

Petit, E., Mougin, F., Bourdin, H., Tio, G., & Haffen, E. (2014). Impact of 5-h phase advance on sleep architecture and physical performance in athletes. Applied Physiology, Nutrition & Metabolism, 39(11), 1230–1236.

Robertshawe, P. (2007). Treating Fibromyalgia With Massage. Journal of the Australian Traditional Medicine Society, 13(3), 151–154.

Ruffin IV, M. T., Nease Jr., D. E., Sen, A., Pace, W. D., Wang, C., Acheson, L. S., Rubinstein, W. S., O'Neill, S., & Gramling, R. (2011). Effect of Preventive Messages Tailored to Family History on Health Behaviors: The Family Healthware Impact Trial. Annals of Family Medicine, 9(1), 3–11.

Salagaras, B. S., Mackenzie-Shalders, K. L., Slater, G. J., McLellan, C., & Coffey, V. G. (2021). Increased carbohydrate availability effects energy and nutrient periodisation of professional male athletes from the Australian Football League. Applied Physiology, Nutrition & Metabolism, 46(12), 1510–1516.

Selk, J., (2009). 10-Minute Toughness: The Mental-Training Program For Winning Before the Game Begins. McGraw-Hill.

Shirzad, M., Tari, B., Dalton, C., Van Riesen, J., Marsala, M. J., & Heath, M. (2022). Passive exercise increases cerebral blood flow velocity and supports a postexercise executive function benefit. Psychophysiology, 59(12), 1–15.

Sun, P., Liu, D., Cheng, R., Zhang, J., Zhao, K., Ye, X., Lai, J., & Wen, W. (2023). Short-Term Benefit from Core Stabilization Exercises in Adolescent Idiopathic Scoliosis: A Meta-Analysis of Randomized Controlled Trials. Health & Social Care in the Community, 1–8.

Tyndall, I., Howe, B., & Roche, B. (2016). Exposure to Progressive Muscle Relaxation Leads to Enhanced Performance on Derived Relational Responding Tasks. Psychological Record, 66(2), 213–222.

Veronica S. Miller, Graham P. Bates, Hydration, Hydration, Hydration, The Annals of Occupational Hygiene, Volume 54, Issue 2, March 2010, Pages 134–136.

Walker, M. (2017). Why We Sleep: Unlocking the Power of Sleep and Dreams. Scribner.

Section II: Psychological

Aaker, J., Bagdonas, N., (2021). Humor, Seriously: Why Humor Is A Secret Weapon in Business and Life. Currency.

Asken, M., Grossman, D. (2009). Warrior Mindset. Warrior Science Publications.

Bazzini, D. G., Stack, E. R., Martincin, P. D., & Davis, C. P. (2007). The Effect of Reminiscing about Laughter on Relationship Satisfaction. Motivation & Emotion, 31(1), 25–34

Bond Chapman, S. (2013). Make Your Brain Smarter. Free Press.

Breuning, L. (2017). The Science of Positivity. Adams Media.

Carroll, P., (2010). Win Forever: Live, Work, and Play Like a Champion. Portfolio/Penguin.

Csikszentmihalyi, M. (2014). Flow and the Foundations of Positive Psychology: The Collected Works of Mihaly Csikszentmihalyi. Springer.

Demirel, H. (2016). Sleep Quality Differs Between Athletes and Non-athletes. Clinical & Investigative Medicine, 39(6), S184–S186.

Frankl, V. (1959). Man's Search For Meaning. Beacon Press.

Goggins, D. (2018). Can't Hurt Me: Master Your Mind and Defy The Odds. Lioncrest Publishing.

Gómez-Romero M, Jiménez-Palomares M, Rodríguez-Mansilla J, Flores-Nieto A, Garrido-Ardila EM, González-López-Arza MV. Beneficios de la musicoterapia en las alteraciones conductuales de la demencia. Revisión sistemática. Neurología. 2017;32:253–263.

Green, C. A. (2018). Complimentary Care: When Our Patients Request to Pray. Journal of Religion & Health, 57(3), 1179–1182.

Haupt, A., Alter, C., Elliott, P., Mansoor, S., Waxman, O. B., & Zorthian, J. (2023). 5 ways to find your new favorite hobby. TIME Magazine, 201(17/18), 14–15.

Howard, P. (2006). The Owner's Manual For The Brain: The Ultimate Guide To Peak Mental Performance At All Ages. William Morrow.

Igono, J. (2022). Own The Pieces: The Heart-Felt Guide To Mental Performance. Dorrance.

Igono, J. (2023). No Missing Pieces: The Athlete's Journal. All Things Performance.

Levitin, D., (2006). This Is Your Brain On Music: The Science of a Human Obsession. Dutton.

Mumford, G. (2016). The Mindful Athlete: Secrets To Pure Peformance. Parallax Press.

Munroe, M. (2003). The Principles and Power of Vision. Whitaker House.

Munroe, M.(2002). Understanding The Purpose and Power of Prayer. Whitaker House.

Munroe, Myles. In Pursuit of Purpose. Shippensburg, PA, Destiny Image Publishers, 2015.

Myers, D., Dewall, C. N. (2015). Psychology (11th ed.). New York, NY: Worth Publishers.

Nelson, J. L. (2011). Express Yourself. Scholastic Parent & Child, 19(1), 52–54.

Neuhaus, C. (2017). The Multi-Media Journal: Diaries are so yesterday. Meet the modern journal: part day planner, part sketchbook, part notebook, part scrapbook, part file cabinet. Saturday Evening Post, 289(6), 16.

Newport, Cal. Deep Work. New York, NY, Grand Central Publishing, 2016.

Olson, J. (2013). The Slight Edge. Green Leaf Book Group Press.

Portman, S. (2020). Reflective Journaling: A Portal Into the Virtues of Daily Writing. Reading Teacher, 73(5), 597–602.

Ramon Mora-Ripoll, Potential health benefits of simulated laughter: A narrative review of the literature and recommendations for future research, Complementary Therapies in Medicine, Volume 19, Issue 3, 2011, Pages 170-177, ISSN 0965-2299.

Ravizza, K., Hanson, T. Heads Up Baseball. United States, McGraw Hill, 1995.

Restak, R. (2013). Laughter and the Brain: Can humor help us better understand the most complex and enigmatic organ in the human body? (Cover story). American Scholar, 82(3), 18–27.

Sedikides, C., Leunissen, J., & Wildschut, T. (2022). The psychological benefits of music-evoked nostalgia. Psychology of Music, 50(6), 2044-2062.

Shashi K Agarwal. Therapeutic Benefits of Laughter. Medical Science, 2014, 12(46), 19-23.

Smyth, A., & Milyavskaya, M. (2021). Mindfully motivated: Can a brief session of mindfulness meditation enhance motivation towards personal goals? European Journal of Social Psychology, 51, 758–772.

Steinberg, D. B., & Simon, V. A. (2019). A Comparison of Hobbies and Organized Activities among Low Income Urban Adolescents. Journal of Child & Family Studies, 28(5), 1182–1195.

Teng, (Mark) Feng. (2020). The benefits of metacognitive reading strategy awareness instruction for young learners of English as a second language. Literacy, 54(1), 29–39.

Tracy, B. (2016). Get Smart! Tarcher Perigee.

Weinberg, R. & Gould, D. (2015). Foundations Of Sport and Exercise Psychology 6th Edition: Human Kinetics.

Wilson, S. (2013, August 06). The benefits of music for the brain [Paper presentation]. 2013 - How the Brain Learns: What lessons are there for teaching?.

Wilson, S. (2013). https://research.acer.edu.au/research_conference/RC2013/6august/8

Yela, J. R., Crego, A., Gómez, M. M. Á., & Jiménez, L. (2020). Self-compassion, meaning in life, and experiential avoidance explain the relationship between meditation and positive mental health outcomes. Journal of Clinical Psychology, 76(9), 1631–1652.

Yovetich N, Dale A, Hudak M. Benefits of humor in reduction of threat-induced anxiety. Psychol Rep, 1990, 66, 51-8.

Zarzycka, B., & Krok, D. (2021). Disclosure to God as a Mediator Between Private Prayer and Psychological Well-Being in a Christian Sample. Journal of Religion & Health, 60(2), 1083–1095.

Section III: Environmental

Anderson, N. (2013). Victory Over The Darkness. Bethany House Publishers.

Brown, Stuart. Play. New York, Avery, 2009.

Benefits of sunlight: a bright spot for human health. (2008). Environmental Health Perspectives, 116(4), A160–A167.

Cobb, E. (2015). Essentials of Elite Performance 2.0 Course Manual. Z-Health Performance Solutions, LLC.

Cox, D. T. C., Shanahan, D. F., Hudson, H. L., Plummer, K. E., Siriwardena, G. M., Fuller, R. A., Anderson, K., Hancock, S., & Gaston, K. J. (2017). Doses of Neighborhood Nature: The Benefits for Mental Health of Living with Nature. BioScience, 67(2), 147–155.

Daily Play Has Benefits for Kids. (2022). USA Today Magazine, 151(2931), 11.

Downs, N. J., Schouten, P. W., Parisi, A. V., & Turner, J. (2009). Measurements of the upper body ultraviolet exposure to golfers: non-melanoma skin cancer risk, and the potential benefits of exposure to sunlight. Photodermatology, Photoimmunology & Photomedicine, 25(6), 317–324.

Emoto, Masuro. The Hidden Messages In Water. New York, NY, Atria Books, 2001.

Francis-Favilla, A.-G. D. (2022). YOUR BODY ON... Sunlight: Soak up the benefits of the sun without getting burned. Scholastic Choices, 37(8), 4–5.

Goulston, M. (2010). Just Listen. American Management Association.

Kerr, James. Legacy. Great Britain, Constable, 2013.

Marc van Almkerk and Gijs Huisman. Virtual Nature Environments Based on Fractal Geometry for Optimizing Restorative Effects. 2018.

Marselle, M. R. (2019). Theoretical foundations of biodiversity and mental well-being relationships. Biodiversity and Health in the Face of Climate Change, 133-158.

Moawad, T. (2020). It Takes What It Takes: How To Think Neutrally and Gain Control of Your Life. Harper One.

Neuhaus, C. (2019). The Quiet Diet. Saturday Evening Post, 291(6), 16.

Shanahan, D. F., Fuller, R. A., Bush, R., Lin, B. B., & Gaston, K. J. (2015). The Health Benefits of Urban Nature: How Much Do We Need? BioScience, 65(5), 476–485.

Simion, R. M. (2015). The Fractal Technique-An Experiential Approach of Fractal Images in Reducing Perceived Stress Through Therapy of Unification. Journal of Experiential Psychotherapy/Revista de PSIHOterapie Experientiala, 18(2).

Thompson, Curt. Anatomy of the Soul. Carrollton, TX, Tyndale, 2010.

Vernon, J. L. (2016). The Path to Self-Actualization. American Scientist, 104(3), 130.

Walsh, B. (2009). The Score Takes Care of Itself: My Philosophy on Leadership. Portfolio-Penguin.

Wilensky, J. (2001). Quiet Zones for Learning. Human Ecology, 29(1), 15.

Willis, C. (2015). A human needs approach to revealing nature's benefits for visitors to the coast. Area, 47(4), 422–428.

Ancillary References

Kusnanto, H., Agustian, D., & Hilmanto, D. (2018). Biopsychosocial model of illnesses in primary care: A hermeneutic literature review. Journal of Family Medicine & Primary Care, 7(3), 497–500.

Koch, R. (2014). The 80/20 Principle and 92 Other Powerful Laws of Nature. Nicholas Brealey Publishing.

Myers, D., Dewall, C. N. (2015). Psychology (11th ed.). New York, NY: Worth Publishers.

National Council for Behavioral Health. (2015). Mental Health First Aid USA. Washington, DC: National Council for Behavioral Health.

Patrick, Y., Lee, A., Raha, O., Pillai, K., Gupta, S., Sethi, S., … Moss, J. (2017). Effects of sleep deprivation on cognitive and physical performance in university students. Sleep & Biological Rhythms, 15(3), 217–225.

Robinson, P., Turk, D., Jilka, S., & Cella, M. (2019). Measuring attitudes towards mental health using social media: investigating stigma and trivialisation. Social Psychiatry & Psychiatric Epidemiology, 54(1), 51–58.

Scheinbaum, Angeline Close, editor. (2018). The Dark Side of Social Media. New York, NY: Routledge.

Sie, R. L. L., Pataraia, N., Boursinou, E., Rajagopal, K., Margaryan, A., Falconer, I., ... Sloep, P. B. (2013). Goals, Motivation for, and Outcomes of Personal Learning through Networks: Results of a Tweetstorm. Journal of Educational Technology & Society, 16(3), 59–75.

Xiang, Z., Tan, S., Kang, Q., Zhang, B., & Zhu, L. (2019). Longitudinal Effects of Examination Stress on Psychological Well-Being and a Possible Mediating Role of Self-Esteem in Chinese High School Students. Journal of Happiness Studies, 20(1), 283–305.

"If your output is greater than your intake, then your upkeep will be your downfall"

-Anonymous

www.ingramcontent.com/pod-product-compliance
Lightning Source LLC
Chambersburg PA
CBHW060356050426
42449CB00009B/1754